NAKHTI QUEEN MOTHERSHIP

Kali J.N.S

Nakhti By Kali J.N.S

*Dedicated to Jali Earl, Mom, Jaqueline,
and the Righteous Ancestors*

CONTENTS

INTRODUCTION

The Nakhti Queen Mothership was born out of a great desire to understand what happened in pre-colonial Africa that led to the colonization of Africa and the trans-Atlantic slave trade. Upon researching my inquiry, I discovered the various cultures, political rulership, values, and a constant stream of consciousness of matrilineality called the Queen Mothership. This concept is found throughout many melanated cultures. I also discovered that this Queen Mothership was overthrown around the same time West Africa embarked on global trade, with slavery and colonization following shortly. The remnants of the overthrow of the Queen Mothership are still felt today. This book will elucidate the history of the Queen Mothership and a call to reinstate the Queen Mothership by Black women understanding the need for healing liberation and enlightenment. The Queen Mothership concept is the natural philosophy of based on balance, logic, spirit, and truth. This book outlines what the Nakhti Queen Mothership will look like and list the benefits, beliefs, and tenants that should be embraced to implement this concept.

CHAPTER 1. WHAT IS THE QUEEN MOTHER SHIP CONCEPT?

During the pre-colonial period, Africa was organized around the authority of chiefs, kings, elders, and Queen Mothers. Queen Mothers were once critical political figures who held power and were even considered to be autonomous rulers. Among certain tribes, there were traditionally male and female counterparts in all aspects of the political and communal hierarchy. This dual rulership created a balance between the divine feminine and masculine principles in all aspects of life, which was believed necessary to make wholesome decisions. The concept of Queen Mothership is described as a dual-sex system. I am not merely discussing gender roles or role reversal. I am talking about pragmatism, mutual respect, and balance between the law of gender.

The Queen Mothership is not synonymous with matriarchy; it merely means that hierarchies, classes, and the domination of one gender by the other did not exist. Instead, the Queen Mothership was multi-level governance with a matrix of ethics to revere the divine feminine, and masculine. Queen Mothers had jurisdiction over women and oversaw any issues that involved both men and women together, such as sexual violence, adultery, marital conflict, and abuse. In addition, the women governed food allotment, medicine, administrative tasks, shamanism, and sometimes military affairs. Black male kings and chiefs were indeed in existence and held a great deal of power, but final decisions for the community were to be made with the Queen Mothers, oracles, and elders. In some instances, Queen Mothers held the final vote.

It is theorized that geographical attributes have contributed to the Queen Mothership. For instance, areas witht tropical weather lead to higher agricultural output. Women oversaw the growing and harvesting of crops and were looked to as the "keepers of the food." They were also in charge of the water supply because they had to water the plants and cook the food. Men were the hunters, craftsmen, warriors, priests, and to a lesser extent, textile makers. The Queen Mothership thrived because women contributed so much to the order of the social system; it was considered unwise for men to maltreat the women, lest they risked the women starting separate communities, doubling the tasks for everyone in the tribe.

I will also argue that there are evolutionary biological attributes for the formation of the Queen Mothership. In this system, the mother was sacred and held unlimited authority. The power of motherhood was symbolized in African and Indigenous traditional religions. For instance, the placenta and blood of childbirth were thought to have great spiritual power. The fact that women breastfed the nation was also an influencing factor during this time. In addition, the menstrual blood was thought to possess power, and in individual kingdoms such as Egypt, Pharaohs would drink menstrual blood for spiritual abilities. In other African Kingdoms, men were forbidden to be around women during the menstrual time to avoid juju (magic).

There are hundreds of thousands of ancient African artifacts of fertility and tantra symbols of the iconography of the Black women with an emphasis on the breast, childbirth, hips, vagina, and buttocks. These artifacts can be found in museums that can be viewed today. Scholars suspect that patrilineality became part of African culture with the introduction from Indo Europeans and Arabs. Patrilineality was implemented after the overthrow of the Queen Mothership occurred, and the trafficking of Black women to Arabs began. This shift was also the beginning of colonial rule.

As a result, Queen mothers lost social, religious, constitutional, and political privileges and rights. I will go into greater detail about the overthrow of the Queen Mothership in chapter two.

Lastly, I will cover examples of this concept in pre-colonial Africa.

CHAPTER 2. HOW THE OVERTHROW OF THE QUEEN MOTHERSHIP LEAD TO OUR DEMISE

When colonists arrived in Africa, they only wanted to negotiate with titled men, not the Queen Mothers. Colonists from Europe believed in patrilineality and brought this mindset into the world trade enterprise.

African male kings and chiefs who would have otherwise been required to consult with the Queen Mothers before making decisions for the entire community no longer felt it necessary after getting involved in global trade. Also, Queen Mothers often warned African kings and chiefs about the dangers of selling rival tribes and prisoners into slavery to foreigners believing that such shortsightedness in rulership would backfire. These same women were killed off or had their power diminished with the help of others in the tribe.

The global trade with foreigners was the first fragment of the dual political rulership between African men and African women. The overthrow of the Queen Mothers began around the time of the slave trade and trafficking of African women and men. African male kings simply wanted total control in their reign to make deals with colonists to sell their people as slaves for material items and goods. However, as colonists' powers ramped up their presence in Africa, it was simply too late to turn the downward course African society had taken from being naive in dealing with foreigners.

The Queen Mothers power further diminished because patrilineal political systems were implemented throughout Africa. To be frank, African men overthrew the Queen Mothership in the hopes of setting up patriarchy with foreign male counterparts so that they could benefit from global trade and rule in bliss. This idea was a grave mistake and one that evidently backfired because they, along with African women, became subjugated under the same system they inadvertently helped to create. These actions descended the fate of other melanated people on other land mass for the last 1000 years with the advent of the trans-atlantic slave trade, pacific slave trade, and colonialism.

The greed and materialism of male chiefs and kings led to the overthrow of the Queen Mothers and oracles. . The overthrow is where the primal hatred and jealousy of the iconography for the architect of the original woman and her essence began; first with her proverbial son who made deals with colonists. This self-hatred spirit has also been internalized by Black women and projected onto one another. The overthrow of the Queen Mothership was the most significant spiritual crime committed, second to the African selling their people into slavery, which descended the melanated race into the abyss globally.

All one needs to do is study what was taking place when West African empires began to fall and think about what happened to Egypt during the Hellenistic Greek Period when Egyptians shared the teachings from their mystery schools and esoteric knowledge. Egypt was conquered, never to be the same. Think about what happened to the Moors 800 year reigned when they started to sell Black women to the Arabians as slaves while simultaneously creating a different race of people. This empire fell as well.

One can still see the remnants of what happened during the reign and fall of the Melanated race by visiting European museums. Currently, there are 2.5 million artifacts from all four corners of Africa in Europe. We must think about how the overthrow of the Queen Mothership affects Africa and other melanated people in other landmasses.

The overthrow gave rise to gender imbalance, enslavement, brainwashing, and self-hatred.

Consequences

Africa, and in particular, West Africa, has never been the same since the overthrow of the Queen Mothership and the slave trade. The descendants of the collaborators that sold their ancestors to slavery are still experiencing the after effects. Moreover, the effects of the conference of Berlin and colonization still have a stronghold on the consciousness and rulership of Africa. The entire diaspora is still hurting as a result.

This chapter only lets the melanated race know how we got into this situation and how being honest about it is the first step to self reflection. To be frank, the naivete, low self-esteem, and sex trafficking of the Black woman led to the squandering of land, resources, and ingenuity. Still, it can be recaptured individually and hopefully in its entirety.

After the overthrow of the Queen Mothership, a malediction was placed upon people of African descent. Malediction in this book means the lesson learning period for wrong past actions. This malediction can easily be broken because it is self-imposed by our ancestors and collective consciousness. However, it is simple and is as follows: "Until the Black man does right to the Black women, his manhood will never prosper, and Until Black people do right by themselves, they will never prosper."

The intricacies of what it means to "do right by the Black woman and to ourselves" are detailed in chapter five, "Tenets of the Nakhti Queen Mothership." Individuals can break the malediction, but it would be advantageous for melanated people to work towards healing collectively.

CHAPTER 3. WHAT IS THE POINT OF THE NAKHTI QUEEN MOTHERSHIP IN THE 21ST CENTURY?

The Nakhti Queen Mothership is a philosophy geared towards enlightening Black women, and with her empowerment, she can evolve her consciousness by serving the Self (soul). This empowerment requires that she puts her survival, liberation, and enlightenment first, and then that of her children. Without her focus on serving the Self, she can make no concerted effort of being in balance, in good health, or a healed human being. Instead, you will have a person who is made wretched and exploited. The only way the Black woman can be of any use to her community is to refuse to sacrifice herself for nothing in return and demands reciprocation for all the energy she expends to others.

The Black woman must take her divine feminine power back through discipline, strategy, and dark feminine energy. After she evolves her consciousness by serving the Self, she can then pass wisdom down to her children and shift the consciousness of a generation, as well as reprogram Black children's epigenetics. I believe that such empowerment of restoring the Queen Mothership philosophy will stem from the Black woman centering the Self (soul) first. Regardless of their ethnicity

This evolution of consciousness requires the reinstatement of the Queen Mothership within the subconscious of Black women so that her standards and quality of life increase. Women are the first teachers of humanity, and if there is an imbalance of any kind with the women, it can ruin an entire generation for centuries. Therefore, the Queen Mothership is a way of life to be taught by the women so that in the future generations, we can remove the toxic elements out of our community, restore the Black women, increase our societal standing and ascend our consciousness as a people.

Black women are at a "great conundrum" in which their community rarely supports them, yet she lives in a system of racial hierarchy. It is up to her to decide what she will do within that "great conundrum," and there is more than one correct answer. The Nakhti Queen Mothership is just one tactic to solve some of the issues Black women face. There is to be no judgment of anyone who disagrees with the Queen Mothership concept, sans if the disagreements lead to threats against our physical well-being.

The list below details twenty reasons why the Nakhti Queen Mothership should exist. It is a philosophy that should be dynamic and based on discipline, precision, truth, logic, and spirit. The Nakhti Queen Mothership aims to:

1. Empower Black women
2. Restore balance and harmony between the feminine and masculine principle
3. Restore balance within child-rearing by becoming the first teachers of our children and promoting inductive learning
4. Restore self-love within Black women
5. Restore balance on planet Earth by promoting a clean environment, the safety of wildlife and the plant kingdom
6. Restore the sisterhood among Black women to have a sustainable and genuine love for one another and ourselves.
7. Restore the image of the Black woman by promoting her natural beauty without seeking validation or approval from society
8. Teach young boys, girls, and adults to take accountability for their community
9. Honor tradition,
10. Become in tune with Nature
11. Stop the abuse, disrespect, and degradation of Black women

12. Raise our standards in our love life and never settle
13. Promote nuclear family units and marriage before having children
14. Promote balanced and healthy manhood that protects and supports the community
15. Practice self-sufficiency
16. To undo centuries of oppressive brainwashing
17. Promote the safety and livelihood of Black women
18. Reset the community and raise a new son that honors the Queen Mother
19. Obtain knowledge needed to activate the light codes in her proverbial "sons" (Black men)
20. Restore the true Nature of the Black man by activating light codes as a baby and in their child-rearing

As a caveat, not everyone will care about this system, and that is okay. The Queen Mothership is a way of life. There will be no proselytizing or convincing adults about the validity of the Nakhti Queen Mothership. For women and men who raise their children with Queen Mothership principles, we can ensure a generation that knows how to love themselves, trust one another, build their community, and appreciate their history and ancestors. The results and efforts of this philosophy may not be realized in our generation, but perhaps by the first and second generation, we can expect to see results! We can review and evaluate the second generation to assess whether a shift in consciousness towards this way of life positively impacts the socioeconomic status, health status, relationships, happiness index, and cultural values of the future melanated generation. Whether you are a single Black person, or married Black couple, it will be up to you to restore the natural balance and power of the Queen Mothership.

CHAPTER 4. THE ADMISSION, PERDITION, AND ALCHEMY

Perdition usually takes place before the alchemical stage. This process alone is often excruciating and can feel like "punishment" (perdition). In other words, no-pain, no-gain. Perdition, in this sense, has to do with the Black women's admissions of her behavior. Admission means to be in acknowledgment and acceptance of the truth.

In the context of Black (eumelanated) womanhood and her history, admission has a precise meaning. What should we be admitting to ourselves as eumelanatewomen? The answer can be found after a keen analysis of the state of various melanated communities and our status globally. A prerequisite to understanding some of the concepts in this chapter includes having a brief knowledge about the twelve laws of the universe, and the definition of alchemy. An online search will do. The answers I give will not be the only ones, but here are a few:

Black women must admit that it was a mistake

to be selfless. Our failure to understand the laws of compensation allowed us to give energy away without reciprocation. The conventional interpretation of the law of compensation means that we are compensated in direct proportion to what we put out into the universe. This law is still present on the micro-level in interpersonal relationships. Instead, we should look at compensation in terms of energy. We should combine it with the law of polarity, which states that everything in the universe has its contrast or opposite, but exists on the same spectrum. It is the very existence of opposites that help us understand the wheel of fortune of life.

Regarding these two laws combined playing out energetically within the interactions of Black women and society, these laws tell us that ALL energy must be reciprocated to maintain balance. In simple terms, whatever you give your energy to, you should receive energy back in kind. The Black woman must understand that energy must be reciprocated. She cannot give her emotional and physical labor, time, resources, and love to the point of being drained without any reciprocation from the community in which she resides regardless of landmass.

The Black woman must understand that energy is to be harnessed in ways that serve her. The habit of self-sacrifice to the point of sacrilege and embarrassment goes against the laws of the universe.Enlightenment through serving the Self (soul) is the only way the Black woman can be whole. This wholeness and balance are the only accurate way to help her community. The Great Ramana Maharshi said, "Your own Self-Realization is the greatest service you can render the world." The Black woman must simply admit that it was a mistake not to practice self care and self love. Only the Black woman can understand this statement as self-evident after analyzing her community, treatment, socioeconomic status, image, and relationships. It is simply not necessary to detail all the woes that lead me to this conclusion.

The second admission is to recognize that we frequently have a subconscious preoccupation with the acceptance, approval, and validation from "societies." This preoccupation simply cannot be tolerated in the Nakhti Queen Mothership. The Black woman has inherent value; it is not based on materialism, degrees, status, or anything in this third-dimensional realm.

The third admission is to recognize the primal energy of jealousy and self-hatred that many Black women possess since the 1000-year demise of her image. To be fair, this energy was manifested by multiple factors that may not be of the Black woman's doing. I argue that it is nothing more than the internalization of projections from others in her society. Nonetheless, the fracture in sisterhood still exists, and while we may not be the cause of the hurt, we are still responsible for healing, and we certainly do not have a right to project that pain onto fellow Black women. Lack of sisterhood inevitably undermines womanhood. The beauty, creativity, and intelligence of Black women become harder to self-actualize if there are other Black women at the forefront spewing hate out of primal jealousy. Black women must move as a phalanx in their quest to restore the Queen Mothership by focusing on what wins and what works best for the sisterhood.

The last admission concerns our "sons" (Black men) in a proverbial sense and the mistakes in raising them. It is no secret that many of these "sons" grow up to have resentment towards Black women, low self-esteem, self-hatred, and disdain for the image of their mothers. It was a mistake not to systematically structure these "sons" child-rearing to eliminate the inauspicious elements we see in our culture. For instance, we should have been more defiant against the tarnishing of our image in hip hop. We should not have coddled our "sons" to their detriment. We should have refused to birth children out of wedlock to men who would not commit to fatherhood. We should have refused to provide resources for grown men. We should have refused to give up the sisterhood for male-identified consciousness.

These are mistakes that have led to the complete breakdown of the nuclear family. This admission is not to solely blame Black women for this breakdown. It is a call to action for a "reset" for what we will allow as women. We must simply acknowledge the mistake and move on to greener pastures. The details of how this child-rearing will be outlined in another book with a few examples presented in chapter nine, but it will require systematic controls and processes that would need to be implemented from the child's birth.

These admissions will be painful and feel like perdition, but it is required for enlightenment. As the Black woman centers herself in her quest for healing, liberation, and knowledge, it will trickle down to her children because she is the mother of humanity. She will need to reset her ecosystem. Failure to reset will harm the future generation of Black girls and boys and continue to lead to our demise. It is through these admissions that real alchemy can take place. I say this with love!

CHAPTER 5. TENETS OF NAKHTI QUEEN MOTHERSHIP

The tenets of the Nakhti Queen Mothership aim to build cultural values centered on self-love, respect, discipline, spirit, balance, logic, precision, and knowledge of Self. Below list the principles:

- Both genders will understand that their roles are complementary, cooperative, pragmatic, compassionate, and built on reciprocation.

- Both genders will recognize the power that the masculine and feminine principles possess and respect their essence equally while understanding that gender roles will be based on pragmatism and what is best for individual families.

- Both genders will understand that the Black woman is the first being on the planet. She is the creator of humanity and the creator of the original Black man. Whose mitochondrial DNA and nine-month incubation period in her womb allow her "son" (Black men) to exist in the third-fifth dimensional realm.

- Both genders will respect their ancestors, Nature, and life.

- Both genders will emphasize the importance of Vitamin D synthesis from the sun due to increased melanin levels and will spend time in the sun.

- Both genders will encourage healthy eating amongst each other and support one another in making lifestyle changes and limiting recreational drugs and alcohol to social activities.

- Both genders will understand that males tend to inherently have more muscle mass than women, thus making it unwise for men to hit women and children physically. Instead, they should use their increased muscle mass to lift heavy items.

- Both genders will understand that Black manhood must be restored and learned anew through the wisdom, mystery sciences, ancestors, elders, and Queen Mothers.

- Both genders should know the basics of human survival at its core. Survival means at least knowing how to live off Nature if needed. This knowledge can be obtained by learning to grow your own food. In addition, survival entails knowing the basics of building an outdoor shelter, knowing how to make a water filtration device, and knowing the basics of clothing the body and keeping warm.

- Both genders will understand that the daughter and son are to be loved and raised with discipline, joy, ethics, high science, and knowledge of Self (soul). Children will embrace education, hard work, community, and creative expression.

- Both genders will understand that children can talk to parents about anything and voice their perspectives with logical reasoning during a discussion.

- Both genders will understand that confidence cannot be built by comparing oneself to others or tearing others down to make yourself feel better.

- Both genders will understand that the Black man must be willing to be enlightened by highly intelligent Queen Mothers, elders, and intergalactic beings.

- Both genders will practice caution against Black women who are jealous-hearted. The Black man should not encourage the gossiping about other Black women for no discernable reason, and no wrongdoing on the part of the Black woman being gossiped about. Instead, he should refer her back to the Nakhti Tenets and remind her of the importance of not defaming her image and sisterhood.

• Both genders will stop holding Black women to ridiculous standards via being overly critical and judgmental for no reason other than jealousy, self-hatred, and primal inferiority complex engendered from being subjugated for the last 1000 years.

• Both genders will understand that the Black man must be willing to sacrifice to protect his manhood.

• Both genders will understand that the Black man must revere and adore the image of his mother and that of his own. He will stand up and never cower.

• Both genders will understand that they should never forgive someone who has no remorse for the wrong they have done to them.

• Both genders will understand that it is imperative to defend themselves if physically attacked by outsiders.

• Both genders will understand the golden rule and the inverse of the golden rule; "Do unto Others As you will want them to do unto you." The equal and opposite of this rule is, "Do unto others as they have done unto you."

CHAPTER 6. WHAT IF IT DOES NOT WORK?

Some may ask, "what if the goal of Nakhti Queen Mothership does not work"? This question can only be answered after one through two generations. One must have measurable and result-oriented controls to answer this question because the Nakhti Queen Mothership exists to contribute to society and the individual. When I talk about controls, I am referring to information and measurement. We can measure if the Queen Mothership works by measuring results against expectations. Such expectations consist of increased marriage rates, increased home economic equity, a decrease in domestic and sexual violence, positive trends in education performance, increased business ownership, an increase in the nuclear family, and an increase in Black women elevation. These are just some factors we can measure, and it is not an exhaustive list. Having logical controls will be the only way to measure the results of the Nakhti Queen Mothership and will take place in the future. Keep in mind that controls have specifications:

(1) they must be meaningful, (2) they must be appropriate, (3) they must be congruent, (4) they must be timely, (5) they must be simple, (6) they must be operational.

If it is determined that results did not meet expectations, we must look at the Queen Mothership concept from its objectives and values. In other words, regardless if it does not work for the future generations and in particular if it does not work for men. The Black woman would have regained her true Nature, increased confidence and understanding of her soul blueprint, and rid her epigenetics of the toxic slugs within her bloodline. The value of the Nakhti Queen Mothership for Black women includes keeping her soul blueprint intact. It solves the "great conundrum" of a Black community that undervalues the Black woman while living in a racist society. While this message aims to affect future generations positively, and while we should do our best to disseminate it to our offspring, we are not responsible for saving any community that does not want to be saved.

CHAPTER 7. SUPPORT FACTORS

I believe that society simply has a vested interest in keeping the Black woman mentally oppressed and unenlightened. Allies are fleeting and should not be expected or sought out. The Black woman must understand that she will have little support in restoring her image and soul blueprint. Her children and like-minded Black women and even some like-minded Black men will support her. The message in this book is for all eumelanated women regardless of where she resides on planet earth. Individuals who adhered to this message should expect to be scrutinized. It has been 1000 years of the eumelanated women sacrificing herself with no reciprocation or loyalty. The energy these actions have created will not be dismantled without a fight, but we will win! We must focus our intention on the Queen Mothership and restoring the nuclear family in a balanced and holistic way. We must rely on each other for support and let no man put us asunder.

CHAPTER 8. SABOTAGE

We must understand that people will try to sabotage the Nakhti Queen Mothership. Humans have a natural tendency to hate things they cannot control or understand. They also tend to be envious of the progress and enlightenment of others. We must be aware of human nature. We must also be mindful of those who did not have a chance to have successful patriarchy in the age of Pisces. They will try to stop us. These attempts will be futile because the planet alignment has moved into the age of Aquarius/Saturn, which is based on logic, information, balance within the law of gender, and the rise of the feminine energy. The rise of the feminine will take place regardless if eumelanated people get on board or not. It is better to be ahead of the curve in this coming age. We must not let counterintelligence, tribalism, or failed patriarchy stop eumelanated communities from building the queen mothership. Staying focus on the Nakhti Queen Mothership is one of the ways to restore balance in the eumelanated communities regardless of land mass.

CHAPTER 9. EXAMPLES OF SYSTEMATIC AND STRUCTURED CHILD REARING

I will provide two examples of controls that can be implemented to structure the child-rearing of eumelanated children. The goal is to shift the consciousness of our cultural value system in one to two generations and to center the Black woman as the mother of the race. The Black woman is the first teacher and must systematically and consciously teach her son and daughter to value her by any means necessary. It is her actions, identity, and sense of self-worth that determine how her children will subconsciously view the archetype of the Black woman. The examples listed are just a view of ways. More standards with be given in the future!

Example 1
"Queen Mother graduates her son into manhood."
The Black Queen Mother must knight the Black man at age 18 by requiring him to take an oath to:

- Protect Black women, by any means necessary
- Provide to the best of his abilities
- Stand up for his human rights at all cost
- Defend his nuclear family.
- Honor planet earth and Nature
- Preserve his sexual prana and express it in healthy ways
- Obtain knowledge and wisdom

This ceremony is to be done in front of at LEAST three witnesses: one male, one female, and one elder. If no elder is present, a child over the age of twelve can witness the ceremony.

Pictures of transitioned ancestors are to be laid out and relics, symbols, or images of ancestors or things of your choosing.

Materials (optional):
- Incense (moldavite, palo santo, frankincense, dragon's blood, Musk, rose) Choose one or more
- An offering of your choosing (for ancestors/ Gods) this can range from snacks, jewelry, hell notes, food, cigars, and alcohol

- Candles (any candle can be used, but it is best to research the color and corresponding metaphysics when selecting a candle)

All participants in the ceremony should wear one of two color combinations

- Red, and Black,

Or

- Red, Black, and White

The eumelanated male child should fast (freshwater and juices) and refrain from sex for at least 10 hours, but no more than 12 hours before his 18th birthday.

On the morning of his 18th birthday, he should take the Kingship bath made with water, sea salt, patchouli, rosemary, bay leaves, turpentine essential oil (3 drops), peppermint oil (6 drops), and lavender oil (8 drops). The mother and father can prepare this bath.

After bathing and putting on the ceremonial clothing, all participants shall enjoy a light breakfast or brunch together. The mother will use a copper staff infused with clear quartz to Knight her son one to two hours after eating. First, he will bend his knee before her and bow his head down. Then, she will traditionally knight him (staff will pass over both shoulders and head) while saying.

"I (insert first and last name) bestow upon your graduation into manhood. You are required to honor your role as King of the universe, protector of planet earth, and original Black man who was birthed from my blood and ancient celestial ancestors. May you prosper and always live up to your full potential for generations to come. You will now take the oath to:

- Protect the Queen Mothers, by any means

necessary
- Provide to the best of your abilities
- Stand up for your human rights at all cost
- Defend your nuclear family
- Honor planet earth and Nature
- Preserve your sexual prana and express it in healthy ways
- Obtain knowledge and wisdom

After he accepts the oath, the family says a prayer, and they can throw a party, relax, or just hang out for the day.

Example 2

Communal policing

This example is theoretical and should not be enacted until our organizing ability is fully realized. However, follow-up will be given when this system can be implemented and if it can ever legally be executed.Reporting Black men who have violated the Queen Mothership law:

What Reasons Should We Report?

Sexual harassment
Serial cheating
Abandoning Children
Physically abusing women and children
Sexual violence
Theft

Why Report?

It is essential to know which community members are unreliable, untrustworthy, dishonest, and emotionally and physically violent. The community can distance itself away from men who offend queen mothership society, and it allows the Black women to "choose better" and avoid procreation and interaction with such characters.

Once a report is filed (usually online), the claim will be investigated by the Queen Mother patrol within 72 hours. The plaintiff should gather all evidence and witness statements as soon as possible to ensure speedy rectification. If the plaintiff faces serious bodily harm and cannot wait 72 hours, she is to call 911 and submit an emergency shelter request. The plaintiff will be sent a stipend for 96-hour (four days) lodging or have lodging booked for her. She will be required to submit a receipt of accommodation as part of the terms and conditions.

The elders of Queen Mothers are to carry out legal retribution against men who undermine the system in traditional fashion. No more than ten Queen Mothers will carry out the retribution. The details of what this retribution entails will not be listed in this book because it is for women initiated into the elders of the Nakhti Queen Mother Ship. However, if it is determined that the offense is true, the community will be made aware of the crime.

CHAPTER 10. QUEEN MOTHERSHIP EXAMPLES IN PRECOLONIAL AFRICA

Examples of the Queen Mother Ship concept can be found in pre-colonial Africa in various clans. These examples lend credence to the premise of the Nakhti Queen Mother Ship and shed light on the Nature of African systems and pedagogy.

Ashanti Women in Ghana

The Ashanti people of Ghana led a battle against British occupation led by Queen Mother Asante Waa of Ejisu. In March 1900, Asante Waa called Ashanti chiefs to take up arms against the British, who had captured Prempeh I, the Asantehene (King), in 1896 and deported him to the Seychelles Islands off the northern tip of Madagascar. The King and 30 of his chiefs and elders were in exile for four years because the Ashanti chiefs in Ghana were scared to wage war against the British. Queen Mother Asante Waa gave an encouraging speech to her army and about 4,000 men to fight against exploitation by the British. Below is the declaration of the Queen Mother:

> Listening to the Voices How can a proud and brave people like the Asante sit back and watch, while the white man took away their King and chiefs and humiliated them with a demand for the Golden Stool. The Golden Stool only means money to the white man; they have searched and dug everywhere for it; I shall not pay one predwan (pound]) to the governor. If you, the chiefs of Asante, are going to behave like cowards and not fight, you should exchange your loin clothes for my undergarments. (Agyeman-Duah & Boateng, 2000, p. 40)

Queen Nzinga of Ndongo and Matamba

Queen Nzinga was a 17th-century Queen of the Ndongo and Matamba Kingdoms of the Mbundu people in what is known as Angola today. Queen Mother Nzinga fought for the freedom and independence of her kingdoms against the Portuguese, who concentrated their efforts towards Southwest Africa in attempts to control the slave trade. Queen Nzinga had to kill her brother and father because they wanted to make deals with the Portuguese and was on the battlefield at the age of sixty-two, with one eye fighting for the rights of her people.

Pre-colonial Igbo Society (Nigeria)

In the Pre-Colonial Igbo Society, there was a belief that a man could not achieve any standing in life without a woman. As a result, the Igbo were a matrilineal people, though male elders, kings, and chiefs were essential to the functioning of society.

Female assertiveness was not deemed socially deviant, and the Igbo men in the community fostered it. The women did most of the administrative work in the village.

In traditional Igbo society, a woman's anger was feared and avoided by the men. The women often united against a man who committed incredulous acts against the community, such as stealing, violence, and excessive lying. He received a spanking on the butt by all the Queen Mothers in the village, and his prized possessions were destroyed. Other Igbo men knew it was no point in coming to the rescue of their fellow man because they believed it was his foolishness that brought the wrath of the women on himself.

Akan

In the Akan tradition, Queen Mothers are the keepers of genealogical knowledge and the high priestesses of the community. They often advise and rule alongside the King or chief and can select candidates for the next chief. Akan Queen Mothers held veto power over the King and can appoint staff. They also have judicial power for disputes brought to the court by women and men. When necessary, these Queen Mothers can assume a war leader position.

Bini

Queen Mothers came into existence after the end of the fifteenth century in the ancient Kingdom of Benin after a battle for the throne. The women won, and Queen Mother Idia became queen of the empire. Queen Mothers of Benin were known as Iyoba. They held had a great deal of power and were revered as the protectors of the kings.

Burundi

In the ancient Kingdom of Burundi, Queen Mothers were known as a *Mugabekazi*. These figures advised the King during their reign. They were usually the biological mother of the King or the stepmother.

Dahomeyan

Amongst the Fon people of Dahomey, Queen Mothers held the title of *Kpojito*. These titleholders presided over the religious ceremonies and served as counsel to the King. This kingdom was also known for its all-women Dahomey Amazon military unit. Even today, Queen Mothers still oversee administrative tasks and serve as the council.

Kongo

In the ancient Kingdom of Kongo, Queen Mothers, known as *Mwene Nzimba Mpungu,* were usually related to the ruling King. She was expected to lead the other women in the kingdom's crown council.

Krobo

Among the Krobo, there is "a chief Queen Mother" and several "lower-level" Queen Mothers ruling under her. It is theorized that the tradition of the Queen Mother may have been adopted from the Akan people of Ghana. The Krobo selected their Queen Mothers through secret elections by the elders. Once a new Queen Mother is chosen, she is made aware of her role by having white clay smeared on her arm. Then, a ritual is performed where she is initiated, given a new name, and then presented to the chief. Thus, Krobo Queen Mothers are "mothers" of their community.

Kushite

In the Kingdom of Kush, a Queen Mother was known as a Kandake. She usually ruled alongside her son or the Qore of Kush. She held priestly duties. Queen Mothers in Kush were also mentioned in both the Alexander Romance and the New Testament of the Bible.

Pabir

In the Pabir tradition, Queen Mothers are expected to become celibate. She is a high priestess, and she has the power to gain allies when she needs to oppose the King.

Serer

In the Serer kingdoms of Senegambia, a Queen Mother was referred to as a *Lingeer*. She was typically the mother or sister of the reigning King, referred to as Lamane. She ruled her territory in the King's kingdom. Also, dynastic succession was vested in the Queen Mothers' progeny instead of the King's.

Swazi

In the Swazi tradition of Southern Africa, the Queen Mother is known as the Ndlovukati. She rules with the King, her son known as Ingwenyama of Eswatini, in a Diarchy. The Ndlovukati is spiritually prominent in rulership. Historically, the Ndlovukati have substantial power. The power of the Ndlovukati serves as a counterweight to that of the Ngwenyama and rival royal princes.

Tswana

Amongst the Tswana people, the Queen Mother is referred to as the *Mohumagadi Mma Kgosi*. She serves as an advisor to the chief and is generally held in high esteem by the community members that he rules.

Yoruba

In the Yoruba tradition, women of varying ages are installed as the "titled mothers of the kings" of the Yoruba. For instance, the Erelu Kuti of Lagos is ranked third in the order of precedence. She serves as regent when the "stool" of the King (Oba of Lagos) is vacant. As part of the coronation ceremonies for a new Oba, she also publicly blesses the candidate before his reign. For these reasons, she is regarded as the Queen Mother of the realm.

In Egbaland, the *Moshade* is responsible for crowning the King (Alake of Egbaland). Following the crowning, she also conducts the installations of all his lower-level chiefs. Due to this, she, too, claims Queen Mother as part of her ceremonial style.

Women in Yorubaland hold the title "Iya oba." There is also a class of women known as *Oba Obirin* or "King of the women" and high-ranking female chieftains called Iyalode. These figures oversee women's affairs in the various kingdoms and represent their gender in the privy councils of the kings.

CITATION

Diop, C. A. (1989). The cultural unity of Black Africa. Lawrenceville, NJ: Red Sea Press.

Fallon, K. M. (1999). Education and perceptions of social status and power among women in Larteh, Ghana. Africa Today, 46(2), 67–92.

Farrar, T. (1997). The queen mother, matriarchy, and the question of female political authority in pre-colonial West African monarchy. Journal of Black Studies, 47, 579–598.

"Inclusion of Queen-mothers in House of Chiefs is Constitutional - Dr. Danaa." My Joy Online. 1 February 2014. Retrieved 4 January 2016.

Kaye, J. (22 June 2009). "Kathleen M. Fallon, Democracy and the Rise of Women's Movements in Sub-Saharan Africa." Canadian Journal of Sociology. 34 (3): 953–955. DOI:10.29173/cjs6330. Archived from the original on 13 January 2018. Retrieved 4 January 2016 – via HighBeam Research

Kies, S. (2013). Matriarchy, the colonial situation, and the women' s war of 1929 in southeastern Nigeria

Ogbomo, W. (2005). "Women, Power and Society in

Pre-colonial Africa." Lagos Historical Review. 5 (1)

McGee, K. (2015). The Impact of Matriarchal Traditions on the Advancement of Ashanti Women in Ghana. The University of San Francisco USF Scholarship: a digital repository @ Gleeson Library | Geschke Center

ABOUT THE AUTHOR

Kali J.n.s

 Kali J.N.S is the Author behind Nahkti Self Redox for Black Women, Nakhti Meditation, and The Nakhti Philosophy. She is the founder of Nakhti University and a scholar. She writes across multiple disciplines that address Black history, philosophy, and sociology. She lives in the rural U.S and prefers a naturist lifestyle. She is a graduate of Buffalo State College, Georgia State University, and Columbia University.